BIG BAD BITERS

Wild Cats

Therese Shea

PowerKiDS press™

New York

Published in 2007 by The Rosen Publishing Group, Inc.
29 East 21st Street, New York, NY 10010

Book Design: Michael J. Flynn

Photo Credits: Cover © Michael Lynch/Shutterstock; p. 5 (lions) © Dan Hare/Shutterstock; p. 5 (cat) © Martin Smith/Shutterstock; p. 7 © Lynn Amaral/Shutterstock; p. 9 © Kondrachov Vladimir/Shutterstock; p. 11 © William Attard McCarthy/Shutterstock; p. 13 © Digital Stock; p. 15 © Keith Levit; p. 17 © Jakob Metzger/Shutterstock; p. 19 © photobar/Shutterstock; p. 21 © Tom Brakefield/Corbis; p. 22 © Holger Ehlers/Shutterstock.

Library of Congress Cataloging-in-Publication Data

Shea, Therese.
  Wild cats / Therese Shea.
      p. cm. — (Big bad biters)
  Includes bibliographical references and index.
  ISBN-13: 978-1-4042-3522-1
  ISBN-10: 1-4042-3522-1 (library binding : alk. paper)
 1. Felidae—Juvenile literature. I. Title. II. Series: Shea, Therese. Big bad biters.
  QL737.C23S532 2007
  599.75'5—dc22
                                  2006014525

Manufactured in the United States of America

Contents

Wild Cats?

When you hear "wild cats," do you think of kittens acting badly? Wild cats are what we call lions, tigers, leopards, cheetahs, and other members of the cat family that live in the wild.

All these animals share features with the smaller cats we have as pets. They have ears that stand up. They walk on padded paws. They have claws that **retract**. They have strong jaws with sharp teeth. They are all meat-eaters. Let's learn about some wild cats with a "bad bite"!

All cats wash their face with their front paws. The cat licks its paw. Then it rubs its face with the wet paw.

Lions

Lions have been called the "king of beasts" for their strong and noble appearance. Lions have yellow-brown fur. Most male lions weigh about 375 pounds (170 kg) and are about 9 feet (2.7 m) long. Female lions, or lionesses, are usually smaller.

Male lions are the only cats that grow **manes**. A mane protects a lion's head and neck during a fight. It turns darker as the lion gets older.

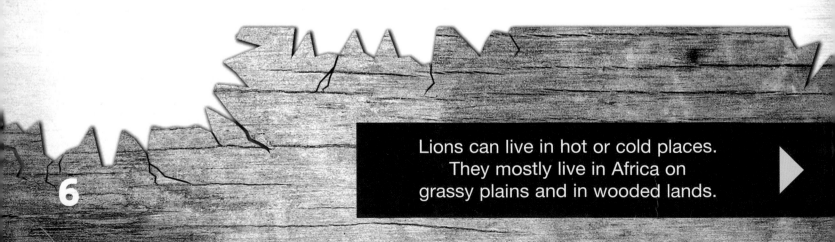

Lions can live in hot or cold places. They mostly live in Africa on grassy plains and in wooded lands.

Lions see well in the dark, so they often hunt at night. Their **prey** include zebra, **antelope**, and buffalo. Lions creep low to the ground to surprise their prey. They throw the animal down and clamp their teeth around its throat. This stops the animal from breathing.

Lions have thirty teeth. Some are for grabbing prey. Some are for cutting through thick skin. Lions don't have chewing teeth. They swallow their food in big pieces.

Lions live in groups called prides. Sometimes several lions hunt together and circle their prey. Lionesses usually hunt for the pride.

Tigers

Tigers once lived many places in Asia. Now tigers are only found in a few places. Like lions, tigers can live in hot or cold places. Unlike lions, tigers like to be in the shade most of the time.

Most male tigers weigh about 420 pounds (191 kg) and are about 9 feet (2.7 m) long. Female tigers, or tigresses, are usually smaller. Tigers have a brown-yellow or orange-red coat. All have black stripes. Some tigers are white with blue eyes.

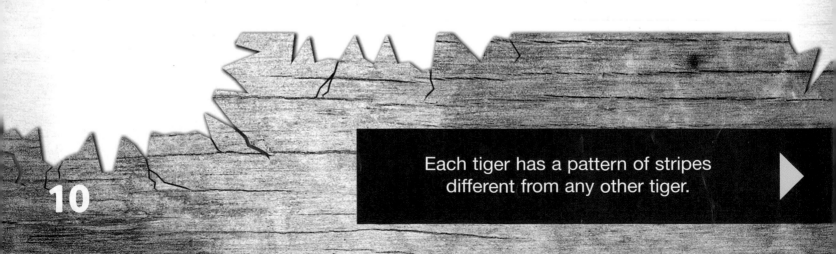

Each tiger has a pattern of stripes different from any other tiger.

11

Tigers usually live and hunt alone. They eat large animals such as deer, antelope, wild cattle and pigs, and even young elephants! They hunt at night and use their good senses of sight, hearing, and smell. They **stalk** their prey or hide and wait. Tigers can run fast for short distances, too. They pull their prey's body to the ground with their teeth just like lions do. After they kill their prey, they drag the body to a safe place to eat it.

Tigers have back legs that are longer than their front legs. This helps them jump long distances.

13

Leopards

Leopards live in parts of Africa and Asia. Most male leopards are about 7.5 feet (2.3 m) long. Female leopards are smaller. Leopards weigh much less than lions and tigers.

Leopards have a light tan coat with many black spots. Leopards that live in the forest are darker than leopards that live in open areas. Their color helps them hide from both enemies and prey. Some leopards are so dark that their spots are hard to see. They are called panthers.

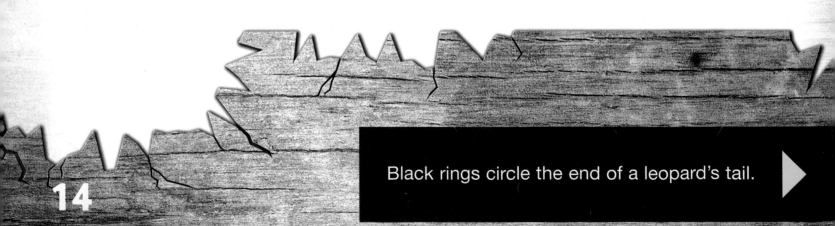

Black rings circle the end of a leopard's tail. ▶

Leopards usually live alone. They hunt animals such as monkeys, antelope, snakes, sheep, and goats at night. They even eat dead animals that they find.

Leopards are different from other big cats because they spend a lot of time in trees. They can see their prey below and jump on them. Once they kill an animal, they may drag it high into a tree. This keeps the prey from being eaten by other animals.

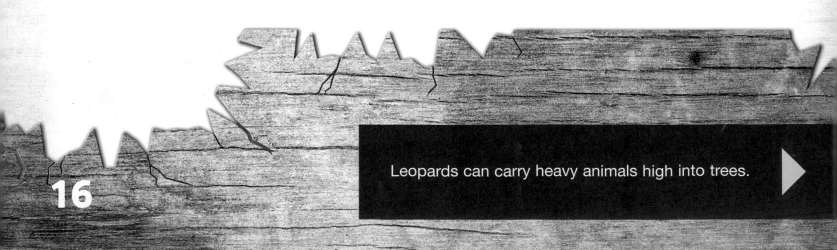

Leopards can carry heavy animals high into trees.

Cheetahs

Cheetahs live on the grassy plains of Africa and parts of Asia. The cheetah is the fastest wild cat. In fact, it is the fastest land animal! Cheetahs can run up to 70 miles (113 km) an hour. That's as fast as a car speeding on a highway!

Cheetahs have a mostly yellow-brown coat covered by black spots. They are usually about 3 feet (.9 m) tall and about 6 feet (1.8 m) long.

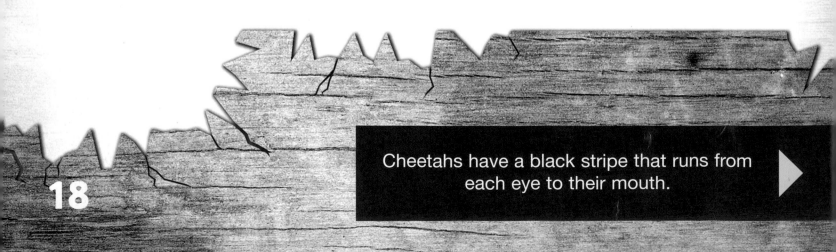

Cheetahs have a black stripe that runs from each eye to their mouth.

Save the Wild Cats

Many kinds of wild cats, like the cheetah, are **endangered**. This means there are not many of them left in the world. People are the wild cats' worst enemy. Some people hunt wild cats for their beautiful skins. Some people have moved onto land where wild cats live. Wild cats are losing living spaces and sources of water and food every day. We must make sure these amazing animals have a place to live and do not disappear forever.

Glossary

antelope (AN-tuh-lohp) An animal much like a deer. An antelope has two horns that stretch upward and backward.

endangered (in-DAYN-jurd) In danger of no longer existing.

mane (MAYN) Long, heavy hair on the head and neck of an animal.

prey (PRAY) An animal that is hunted by another animal as food.

retract (rih-TRAKT) To pull back or in.

stalk (STAWK) To hunt slowly and quietly, without being seen.

warthog (WORT-hawg) A wild hog found in Africa that has two tusks. Male warthogs have wartlike growths on their face.

Index

A
Africa, 14, 18
Asia, 10, 14, 18

C
cheetah(s), 4, 18, 20, 22
claws, 4
coat, 10, 14, 18
cubs, 20

E
ears, 4
endangered, 22
enemy(ies), 14, 22

F
fur, 6

H
hunt, 8, 12, 16, 20, 22

K
"king of beasts," 6

L
leopards, 4, 14, 16
lion(s), 4, 6, 8, 10, 12, 14
lionesses, 6

M
mane(s), 6
meat-eaters, 4

P
panthers, 14
paws, 4
prey, 8, 12, 14, 16, 20

S
skins, 22

T
teeth, 4, 8, 12
tigers, 4, 10, 12, 14
tigresses, 10

Web Sites

Due to the changing nature of Internet links, PowerKids Press has developed an online list of Web sites related to the subject of this book. This site is updated regularly. Please use this link to access the list:
http://www.powerkidslinks.com/biters/wildcats/